12/05

W9-AWA-385

Reading Essentials
in Social Studies

SYMBOLS OF A NATION

The Vietnam Veterans Memorial

Thomas S. Owens

Perfection Learning®

Editorial Director: Susan C. Thies
Editor: Mary L. Bush
Book Design: Emily J. Greazel, Tobi Cunningham
Cover Design: Mike Aspengren

For Richard B. Tomhave—we are so glad you came home.

Acknowledgments

The author is grateful for the assistance of Jan C. Scruggs,
Founder and President of the Vietnam Veterans Memorial Fund,
and Tricia Edwards, the Fund's Program Director.

IMAGE CREDITS
© CORBIS: pp. 5, 12–13, 22–23; © Maury Englander: pp. 10, 11;
Gary Kleber: pp. 35, 36–37

ArtToday (some images copyright www.arttoday.com): pp. 26 (bottom), 30, 42,
42–43, 46; Corel Professional Photos: cover, p. 1; © Dan Arant/VVMF: pp. 31,
32; Mary Bush: pp. 38–39, 40–41; Emily J. Greazel: pp. 2–3, 27; Jacy Johnson:
Wall background, pp. 26 (top), 28; National Archives: pp. 6–7, 8, 9, 15, 16–17,
18–19; Library of Congress: pp. 7 (top), 29; © VVMF: pp. 20–21, 25, 33, 36

Printed in the United States of America.
For information, contact
Perfection Learning® Corporation
1000 North Second Avenue, P.O. Box 500,
Logan, Iowa 51546-0500.
Phone: 1-800-831-4190
Fax: 1-800-543-2745
perfectionlearning.com

1   2   3   4   5   BA   06   05   04   03   02

ISBN 0-7891-5871-x

TABLE OF CONTENTS

Chapter One

What Was Vietnam?

The Vietnam War lasted from 1957 to 1975. It was the longest war in which the United States has ever participated. This lengthy war has a lengthy history.

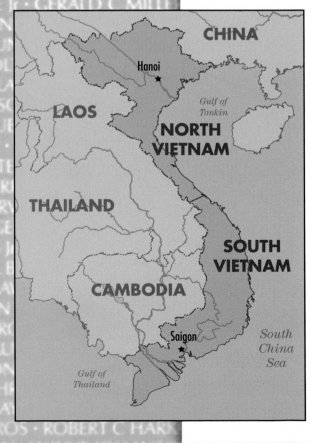

North and South Vietnam

After World War II, a Southeast Asian country called Indochina was ruled by France. But Indochina wanted its independence. In 1946, an eight-year battle started between France and the people of Indochina.

Indochina's soldiers were led by Ho Chi Minh (ho chee MIN). After his forces drove out the French in 1954, Minh became a **national** leader.

During peace talks, Indochina was divided into North Vietnam and South Vietnam. Minh would head a **Communist** government in North Vietnam. Ngo Dinh Diem (NAGO din dee-YEM) became president of South Vietnam. Diem called South Vietnam a **democracy**.

However, South Vietnam's democracy wasn't very democratic. Diem and his family actually controlled the country. They made the rules and set restrictions for the citizens. In 1956, Diem canceled local elections and appointed his own leaders.

Some people living in South Vietnam wanted to overthrow Diem's government. They wanted Ho Chi Minh to lead the entire country. This group was called the Viet Cong. Fighting between the Viet Cong and supporters of the South Vietnamese government started what became known as the Vietnam War.

Ho Chi Minh

Who Was Charlie?

The U.S. military used an alphabet code to spell out abbreviations. V.C. meant Viet Cong. But instead of saying "V.C.," soldiers often said "Victor Charlie" or just "Charlie."

Ngo Dinh Diem

The peace talks that divided Vietnam had also set a date for an election to reunite the country. In 1956, the North and South Vietnamese were to vote and choose one government and one leader. But Diem stalled. He was scared of losing an election to the popular Minh. No election was ever held. Diem's opponents decided that war was the only way to replace him.

Diem's Death

In 1963, Ngo Dinh Diem was murdered by a group of his own generals. South Vietnam was then run by various military groups and leaders. When the war was over, Ho Chi Minh became the leader of the new Vietnam.

How Did America Become Involved in the War?

After World War II, the American government feared the rise of **communism** in Asia and Eastern Europe. Americans were afraid that the Soviet Union, China, and other Communist countries would work together to control the world. Some American leaders talked about the "domino theory." They believed that if one country "fell" to communism, other countries would follow like dominoes. If Vietnam became a Communist country, what was to stop all of Southeast Asia from falling to communism?

The United States felt that it was its duty to protect the world from communism by helping South Vietnam in its fight against Communist North Vietnam.

Sending Support

The first American military arrived in South Vietnam in 1950. These men were not there to fight but only to train, supply, and advise South Vietnamese forces. America called these 35 men a "Military Assistance Advisory Group."

The American "advisors" supported South Vietnam. North Vietnam got money and weapons from the Soviet Union, China, and other countries. Vietnam was a small country, but it was part of a big struggle over the spread of communism. Therefore, both sides received support from powerful countries.

More and more advisors were sent to support South Vietnam. Some of these advisors were killed in accidents or other war-related incidents. In 1961, the first Americans died in active fighting. After that, American troops continued to arrive in Vietnam.

The U.S. military officially ended its "advisory campaign" on March 7, 1964. An estimated 50,000 Americans had already served in Vietnam by that time. Two hundred and sixty-four general **infantrymen** (GIs) had been killed. More than 1,600 had been wounded.

On June 8, 1965, President Lyndon Johnson officially approved the use of U.S. troops in direct **combat**. Battles raged on land, water, and air. Fighting spilled into the countries next to Vietnam.

Lyndon Johnson

NUS · ANTONIO MORALES Jr · RICHARD D WEEDER · ROBERT J NAGY ·
LD · WALTER PLATOSZ · EUGENE E PUER · GARLAND J RANDALL ·
N REECE · ALLAN V REI
1 · CHARLES E SILLAW
WNSEND · ANTHONY
AUDE C BETTY · JOSE
R COCKRELL · ROBERT
OMAN · DELBERT W H
GELS · TERRY H FENE
O McKNIGHT · DON
EN · ROBERT L PITT

Peace?

By the late 1960s, America's involvement in the Vietnam War had become increasingly unpopular in the United States. The first peace talks were held in Paris in May 1968. But by 1969, America's troops in Vietnam peaked at 543,482.

At last, in January 1973, North Vietnam, South Vietnam, and the United States agreed to a **truce** under the Paris Peace Accords. By April of that year, 587 American prisoners of war (POWs) were released. Some had been captured and held for as long as ten years. Later that year, America removed all of its ground troops from Vietnam.

After the United States pulled out of the war, North and South Vietnam continued to fight. Finally in 1975, the Communists gained control of the country. The fears of past American leaders came true. By 1976, the country was unified into one Communist Vietnam.

The United States felt the effects of the war for many years. It is estimated that America spent $150–$200 billion on the war. Nearly 3.5 million American military members spent time in Southeast Asia. More than 58,000 Americans died in Vietnam.

The human costs would be felt for years to come.

Chapter Two

The War in 🦅 America

While the war in Vietnam raged into the 1960s, fighting took place in America as well. This war was one of words and emotions.

The two sides of this "war at home" were called the *hawks* and the *doves*. Hawks were Americans who supported the fight against communism in Vietnam. Doves were citizens who wanted American troops out of Vietnam. They created the peace movement.

The Peace Movement

Many groups wanted the war stopped. Some were ordinary citizens who were simply against U.S. involvement in a **foreign** war. Others were men **drafted** into the army and forced to serve in a war they didn't believe in. Some thought the United States was fighting on the wrong side of the war. **Pacifists** opposed all wars and worked toward finding peaceful solutions.

One group of protesters was called *hippies*. Hippies were people who protested society's traditional ways. They were against wars and

Hippies

discrimination. For several years, the Vietnam War was a focus of hippie protests.

Peace protesters questioned the war. They used words and actions to voice their concerns about America's role in Vietnam. Some of these protests were peaceful, and some were not.

In Favor of the War

Americans who were in favor of the war held their own protests. They vowed to support the U.S. military and its leaders in any way necessary. They believed in the fight against communism. Patriotic bumper stickers reading "My Country—Right or Wrong" and "America: Love It or Leave It" expressed their beliefs.

Protests

Draft Cards

Draft cards were proof that a male had registered with the military. During the time of the Vietnam War, the law required young men to carry their draft cards with them at all times. But young men who were against the war or the draft started burning their cards in public as a sign of protest. Crowds gathered on college campuses to burn draft cards.

Men gather to burn their draft cards.

Music

The protest movement used music as a weapon too. Radios played songs of protest. Some tunes seemed like gentle folk songs, while others spoke harshly of the death and destruction of war.

Rallies

In 1968, protesters gathered outside the Democratic National Convention in Chicago. Democrats at the convention were trying to choose a candidate for president. Vietnam War protesters were joined by other groups protesting against discrimination in America. The protests turned to fighting. Riots spilled into the streets.

A Woman of Peace

In 1916, Jeanette Rankin was the first woman elected to Congress. Rankin was a pacifist who voted against U.S. involvement in both World War I and World War II. She was also very active in promoting children's and women's rights.

In Washington, D.C., that same year, 87-year-old Jeanette Rankin led a peace march of 10,000 women. The Jeanette Rankin Brigade pressured Congress to end the war.

Some protests turned deadly. At Kent State University in Ohio on May 4, 1970, National Guard troops couldn't control an antiwar protest. Guardsmen panicked after the crowds threw rocks and bottles at them. Four students were killed. Most of the Guardsmen sent to stop the riot were as young as the college students themselves.

One week later, 800,000 people attended a protest rally in Washington, D.C. This was one of the larger rallies that occurred during the peace movement.

On January 15, 1968, thousands of women marched from Union Station to the Capitol to present their opinions at the opening of a Congressional session. Ms. Rankin is fourth from the right in the first row.

The protests continued into the 1970s. More than 2,000 Vietnam **veterans** protested in Washington, D.C., in April 1971. They camped out just a quarter of a mile from the Capitol. Many threw away their military medals in front of a statue of Supreme Court Chief Justice John Marshall. Gold Star Mothers joined this march.

Spying on the "Enemy"

In 1970, *Washington Monthly* magazine reported that the army was using secret agents to spy on peace protests. The magazine claimed that nearly 1,000 agents were located in about 200 different places. Hundreds of Americans were being watched in secret—even some members of Congress! When the U.S. Senate held hearings about the spying, the army was ordered to stop.

On March 30, 1971, the army issued secret orders to censor personal mail sent to soldiers in Vietnam. Any letters that contained antiwar material were taken or destroyed.

As the cost of the war continued to climb and the death toll increased, more and more Americans began to question the United States' role in the war. The gradual drop in public support for the war eventually led to the end of America's involvement in Vietnam. But in the meantime, battles continued both at home and in Asia.

Gold Star Mothers

American Gold Star Mothers is an organization of women who lost sons or daughters in any wars that have occurred since World War I. The name "Gold Star" comes from the gold stars that families used to hang on their windows to show that they had lost a family member in a war. The purpose of the group is to support one another and the American ideals for which their children died.

Chapter Three

American Soldiers

N ot every soldier chose to serve in Vietnam. Many physically fit American males age 18–25 were drafted, or forced, into military service. From 1964 to 1973, the American government drafted 1,857,304 men.

The Lottery

Once a young man was 18½, he was old enough to be drafted. Early in the war, local draft boards picked the oldest males first, starting with 25-year-olds. A younger man could spend more than six years wondering if (or when) he'd be chosen.

The marines deliver military aid to South Vietnam.

15

This method of drafting changed in 1969. On December 1 of that year, a lottery drawing was held at the Selective Service National Headquarters in Washington, D.C. The lottery was to see who would be drafted in the year 1970.

Young men born between 1944 and 1950 were of draft age in 1970. Many of them watched the draft lottery live on TV or listened on the radio.

For the lottery, every date of the year was written down and put into a blue plastic capsule. There were 366 capsules in all. (February 29 was included.) The capsules were placed in a large glass container and then drawn out by hand.

Congressman Alexander Pirnie of the House Armed Services Committee drew out the first blue capsule. The date inside was September 14. This meant that all men born on September 14 from 1944 through 1950 would be given the number 1. They would be the first draftees called to serve in 1970. The drawing continued until all days of the year had been paired with numbers.

Staying Out of the War

Some men were not included in the draft.

Before 1971, any man enrolled in college could avoid being drafted. Then the law was changed. Starting in 1971, a student who was drafted was only allowed to finish the current semester before reporting for military duty.

Other types of **deferments** kept men from serving. Ministers were **exempt** from the draft. If a young man could prove that he was the only source of money for his elderly parents, he'd escape the draft.

Some men declared themselves "conscientious objectors" (COs). This meant that they would not serve in the military because of their religious or moral beliefs. COs had to work in alternative public service jobs for the years they would have been called to serve. Many COs worked in hospitals, nursing homes, and poverty programs.

As the Vietnam War lasted longer and longer, the number of COs grew. During World War II, only 1 in every 600 men was a CO. In 1972, there were 130 COs for every 100 active soldiers. This increase in conscientious objectors was another indication of the controversy surrounding the Vietnam War. Even so, the total number of Vietnam COs is guessed to be just 10,000—a small number compared to men who avoided the draft in other ways.

In the earlier years of Vietnam, many young men didn't know how to become COs. Instead, they ran away to avoid the draft, often to Sweden or Canada, which were **neutral** countries. This was against the law. No one knows for sure how many men left, but estimates range from 50,000 to 100,000 men.

Those Who Served

The average age of servicemen in Vietnam was 19. Although males had to be 18 to be drafted, a 17-year-old could **enlist** in the military with his parents' permission.

Many young men who served in Vietnam went to **units** where they knew no one. Trainees would meet at basic training and then be separated. Often there wasn't much time to get to know people once soldiers were in country. "In country" was what soldiers called being in Vietnam. An attack might come before a soldier had even learned the names of the people fighting beside him.

The Vietnamese people were strangers too. American soldiers had to be suspicious of everyone. Soldiers learned quickly that anyone could be a member of the Viet Cong. Many Viet Cong dressed in plain clothes, not in military uniforms. Women, children, and the elderly sometimes helped the rebels. Anybody could be an enemy.

The life of a soldier in Vietnam was harsh. Bombings and enemy attacks were constant. Chemicals used to force Vietnamese soldiers out of forests had immediate and long-lasting effects. Death and injury surrounded soldiers every day.

Coming Home

When the war was over, the weary soldiers returned home. But unlike in previous wars, their homecoming wasn't a celebration of pride, respect, and **patriotism**. Instead, the soldiers were blamed for failing to win the war or for acts of violence committed during the war. Many were simply ignored or rejected.

The war left many veterans with physical and emotional problems. For many years, America was not sympathetic or helpful to these veterans.

Over time, America realized its mistakes in Vietnam and on the home front. Soldiers who were once tormented were eventually honored. But it took time to heal the wounds left by the war. One soldier's dream of a memorial would help this healing process.

Feared Abbreviations

Soldiers and their loved ones back in America feared seeing these abbreviations next to anyone's name.

WIA —Wounded in Action
KIA—Killed in Action
MIA—Missing in Action

An American soldier in Vietnam

Chapter Four

A Soldier's Dream

Jan Scruggs was an American teenager serving in Vietnam. Fresh out of high school, he was a **corporal** and a **rifleman**. He fought. He watched other young men die. Then, during an **ambush**, Scruggs was hit by **shrapnel**. The young man came home. He found an office job with the U.S. Department of Labor and tried to have a normal life again.

A few years later, in 1979, Scruggs went to see a popular movie, *The Deer Hunter*. The movie was about the Vietnam War and how hard life was for many veterans who returned home.

That night, Scruggs couldn't sleep. He tried to remember the names of the men he had fought with in Vietnam. He tried to remember those who had not come back. More than half the men in his unit had been killed or wounded.

Scruggs remembered coming home from Vietnam. No parades had celebrated his return. People had not welcomed him and other returning soldiers. Some protesters had spit on the war veterans. They'd treated the soldiers like evil killers.

He and the other soldiers had been confused. After all, they had simply obeyed the draft and followed orders. They'd thought they were helping America.

The movie had made Scruggs remember. Was America ready to remember too?

Dreams for a Memorial

In the morning, Scruggs told his wife about his plans. He imagined a memorial in Washington, D.C. He wanted a place to display all the names of the Americans who had died in the war.

Scruggs shared his dream at a meeting of Vietnam veterans. He said he wanted to build the Memorial

On May 28, 1979, Jan Scruggs held a press conference to announce the plan to build a national memorial dedicated to those who served in the Vietnam War.

with money from the people—*not* money from the government. If the American people gave money, it would be like the welcoming parade the veterans had wished for but never received. To start the process, Scruggs pledged $2,800 of his own money.

Raising Money for the Memorial

Spreading the word and asking for money was a slow process at first. After two months, the fund-raising effort had gained just $144.50. And the Memorial still needed a location.

Scruggs knew that Congress could donate the land if enough senators agreed to it. So he personally spoke to all the senators, describing his plans. He was surprised to find that people liked his idea.

"Getting government support was easy enough to figure out," Scruggs remembered. "Just getting the attention of senators and staffers was enough."

As a result of Scruggs' efforts to inform the public about his idea, the fund for the Memorial grew. More than 650,000 people donated $10 or less.

View of the Lincoln Memorial, Washington Monument, and Vietnam Veterans Memorial

Children were some of the biggest supporters of the Memorial. A third-grade class from Pottstown, Pennsylvania, sold T-shirts honoring Mike Frey. Frey was a Vietnam veteran whose injuries paralyzed him at age 19. The class raised more than $1,000 through their fund-raising.

Scruggs heard from an entire school in Matoon, Illinois. "Each gave 25 cents to The Wall," he remembered. The students also wrote letters asking their congressmen to support the effort.

By the time Congress had approved the use of two acres between the Lincoln Memorial and the Washington

Monument, the fund-raising group had raised more than $8 million. A contest was then held to decide how the monument would look.

Joy and Tears

Some veterans didn't like the winning design. Their protests threatened to stall the building of the Memorial.

But Scruggs had vowed that a tribute to all Vietnam veterans could be built in three years. He pushed to meet the deadline. To calm protesters, Scruggs agreed to add a more traditional statue to the Memorial's design. And so on Veterans Day weekend in 1982, the completed Vietnam Veterans Memorial was dedicated.

A crowd of 150,000 witnessed the ceremony. There was joy in honoring loved ones. There were tears for those who were lost. There was unity in the gathering. It was exactly what Jan Scruggs had seen in his dreams.

Since then, Scruggs remains a regular visitor to the Memorial. "I go there often since I need to monitor [The Wall's] care and condition," he said. "Each time I try to enjoy its **majesty** and observe the public—particularly school kids—and their reaction to The Wall."

Scruggs always remembers to check panel 16 West, line 45. There, he finds the name of Michael Hrutkay. A fellow infantryman, Hrutkay had laid down a cover of rifle fire so Scruggs and his **comrades** could escape from an ambush. Hrutkay had died to save others in his unit. Because of Michael Hrutkay, Jan Scruggs lived to dream of a memorial to honor his comrade and all soldiers of the war.

Chapter Five

A Student's Vision

The designer of the Vietnam Veterans Memorial wasn't old enough to vote when the war ended. She knew little about the war. But her vision would forever change how others remembered the war.

The Contest

When Memorial Fund members finally knew that there would be a place for the Vietnam Veterans Memorial, they decided to hold a contest. Anyone could enter an idea for the Memorial's design. Professional architects and designers would judge the contest.

The contest had four main rules.

1. The Memorial must contain all the names of the dead and missing.
2. The Memorial must not make a **political** statement.
3. The Memorial must be **harmonious** with the site.
4. The Memorial must be **contemplative** in nature.

The contest received 1,421 entries, which was more than anyone had expected. The entry fee was $20. The prize was $20,000 and the fame of seeing your work stand in a city of monuments.

The Winner

Maya Ying Lin, a 20-year-old senior at Yale University, won the competition. She created the design as a clay model for a classroom assignment. She later said she worked less than six weeks on the design.

The Vietnam Veterans Memorial Fund announces their unanimous selection for the Memorial. Maya Lin displays her winning design for The Wall.

Visitors at The Wall

Lin used the words *visual poetry* to describe her creation. She didn't specifically study the Vietnam War itself for her design. Instead, she thought about the idea of war and how it affects people's lives.

She also went to see where the Memorial would stand. "I had an impulse to cut open the earth," she later wrote, "an initial violence that in time would heal."

Lin imagined two long walls of black **granite**. The walls would meet, forming a shape like the letter V.

A memorial wreath left at the The Wall

The names of the soldiers would be carved into the shining granite. The stone would reflect the faces of the living who came to the Memorial, connecting them to the names of the dead.

Every contest judge chose Lin's design. But when the world saw the plan, many people disagreed with the judges.

Controversy Surrounding the Choice

Since The Wall's foundation would be dug into the ground, some people thought the Memorial would seem like a tombstone. Digging would also hide the Memorial, they said.

Other critics wanted to know why *black* granite would be used. Some people thought black was a sad color.

Most of all, people didn't expect a war memorial to look like Lin's Wall. No soldiers would be shown. No weapons would be displayed. Not even an American flag would fly. Lin's memorial would only feature the names of the dead. And what about the soldiers who had survived?

Some Vietnam veterans worried because Lin wanted to list the soldiers' names by their years of death. The veterans thought that visitors might become frustrated. They could spend hours searching through the more than 58,000 names on The Wall, trying to find the soldier they knew. The veterans wanted the names listed alphabetically.

The wall panel (left side) lists names including:

FREDERICK J FORTNER · ROBERT E FUQUA Jr · MICHAEL J GALLAGHER ·
STANLEY D GILBERT · VERLAND A GILBERTSON · WILLIE V GOREE ·
CHRISTOPHER E HERDERICK · DONALD W HOLLEDER · ALLEN D JAGIELO ·
CHARLES L KENNEDY · JOHN D KRISCHE · JERRY D LANCASTER ·
N · JOE LOVATO Jr · ANDREW P LUBERDA · EMIL G McGIVERON ·
US · ANTONIO MORALES Jr · RICHARD D WEEDER · ROBERT J NAGY ·
· WALTER PLATOSZ · EUGENE J PUER · GARLAND J RANDALL ·
REECE · ALLAN V REILLY · HARRY C SARSFIELD · JACK W SCHRODER ·
CHARLES E SILLAWAY · LUTHER A SMITH · THEODORE D THOMAS Jr ·
SEND · ANTHONY J VAICKUS Jr · JOE D MOULTRIE · KENNETH P WILSON ·
DE C BETTY · JOSEPH O BOOKER · JIMMY MAC BRASHER ·
OCKRELL · ROBERT H DECKER · NATHAN JOHNSON Jr · ALLEN E FIRTH ·
AN · DELBERT W HAASE · JERRY RAY HALL · JACK M HAMMOND ·
LS · TERRY H FENENGA · JAMES S KELL · OWEN C KELLEY ·
McKNIGHT · DONALD T SLUDER · LOUIE OCHOA · HOWARD OGDEN Jr ·
· ROBERT E PITTMAN · ALLEN J ROY · MICHAEL J SIGSBEE ·
· RICHARD M WOYNARSKI · DENNIS G BLACKMON · GREGORY L BROWN ·
M · GLENN G JACKS · DUDLEY N JORDAN · KENNETH D KREHBIEL ·
Y · GERALD W McMILLAN · JOHN F McNAMARA · GARY P POLLEY ·
WILL · CARL A BALLENGER · GEORGE E CLARK Jr · WAYNE A COLANTUONO ·
STANLEY D GUBBELS · WILLIAM H JETT · PAUL E LATOURETTE ·
· GERALD S RYAN · JOHN A RYAN Jr · STANLEY W THOMPSON ·
· WILLIAM L CUMMINGS · DONALD P YARKINGTON Jr · JOHN L JONES ·
· GERALD C MILLER · JEFFREY L MORRIS · PETER J PAELE ·
NETH E TREADWAY · DAVID E WARD · MICHAEL A WYRICK ·
NG · WAYNE M CARDINAL · FRANK B DUNFORD III · JAMES E DOOLEY ·
· THOMAS L GRIFFEE · BARTON E HAYNES · JAMES R JONES ·
WRENCE J STARK · JAMES M McCORMICK · LARRY RAY McDUFFIE ·
ON · JOHN J RHODES · ROGER D ROMINE · DANIEL J RYAN ·
· JOHN F TERRY Jr · WAYNE F WHITEMAN · RUSSELL L ADAMS ·
WARREN D CAMPBELL · KENNEY D CHAPPELL · GEORGE H COLBERT ·
ELLA · MICHAEL C ETTZ · DAVID W FISHER · WILLIAM FORD ·
RELL · LEROY HOPKINS Jr · MICHAEL E LAVALLEE · RAYMOND T MASHI ·
AY · CHARLES E MULLIS · RODNEY W McLEAN · JOSEPH P PINK ·
R III · ROBERT F SHAW · ROBERT J SIME · JOSEPH SOSINSKI ·
· ROBERT G TSCHUMPER · EDDIE D TURNER · GEORGE M VINEYARD ·
ROWNING · RICHARD C CLARK · GARY L CONAWAY · VAUGHN P FLIZANE ·
WKINS · ROBERT D JESSEN · THOMAS S JONES · FREDDIE JOE KEELEY ·
Jr · GILBERT G MARCUM · KEITH A McENANY · RICHARD L McNEISH ·
ODRIGUEZ · BASIL L SAUNDERS · JOEL L SCHUBERT · HAROLD J SOTZEN ·
· MICHAEL C TOSH · SIMEON ANDRADE TUAZON Jr · GAROLD T WILSON ·
N · AQUILLA F BRITT · GREGORY J CANDLER · PATRICK J CARNELL ·
ISCOE · DONALD G STAYROOK · CHARLES A DAVIS · DONALD R FOSTER ·
· JAMES E GISH · GORDON J GRAHAM · MORRIS GRAHAM ·
S · ROBERT C HARKINS · DON C HARRELL · JAMES E HENSLEE ·
· WAYNE JOHANSON · RICHARD A JOHNSON · JEFFREY M KROMMENHOEK ·
SE · DONALD S MOSES · ROBERT E MUSSELMAN · ELEC McCOY ·
LIVER · CHRIS A TOTORA · LAVERN L SALZMAN · CARL S THORNE-THOMSEN ·
· ELMER R L ABLES Jr · RICHARD J ACEVEDO · DAVID A BARTLETT ·
TT · RUSSEL D BENTSON · LARRY D BLEEKER · RICHARD K BOYD Jr ·
· JOHN O COOPER III · ROBERT B CRANE · ALEXANDER N DI GUARDIA ·
AVID S GRIFFIN · SAMUEL L HUNT · GERALD H SLINGERLAND ·
· JOHN J LAWENDOWSKI · CONVERSE R LEWIS III · JOHNNY MEANS ·
RNE · STEPHEN F PETERS · DANIEL P KEE III · STEVEN A SMITH ·
RLIN · STANLEY W TUNALL · BILLY R WOHLGAMUTH · DUANE C AKKERMAN ·
GERSTEIN · ALLEN L ARTHUR · RODGER G BARNES · GEORGE P BARRETT ·

CURTIS E STIEFERMAN · SANDERS
JERRY LEE WIGGINS · GLEN R WILLI
RALPH L FORD · EMMITT R GEORGE
CHARLES K JOHNSTON · RICHARD
LUTHER E PRESTON · CLIFFORD W
RALPH L AVERY · ROBERT J BICKEL
JOAQUIN PALACIOS-CABRERA · RO
RUFUS J DOWDY · DEWAIN V DUB
IRA L GARNER · ROY A GIBSON · RO
CLARENCE JACKSON · LINWOOD C
BRADFORD S KING · RICHARD F L
CLARENCE A MILLER Jr · LOUIS C M
ELBERT F PRICE Jr · ROBERT B REED
RALF L SAUNDERS · CLARENCE W S
MARTIN F STERUD · EDRICK K STEV
GLENN E WHITE · TERRY D WILLIAM
BILLIE JOE BARNETT Jr · EDWARD E
DAVID E CALKINS · JOSEPH McLEM
WILLIAM C DIEHL Jr · LEE A DIXON ·
JACK P LANGLINAIS · WILLIAM W LI
DENNIS J MOORE · EUGENE MORR
RONALD H PAYNE · JESSE J PEARSO
FREDERICK J SEBERS · CLARENCE L S
ROBERT F STRYKER · ESTEBAN W TAI
ROBERT S WALSH · MELVIN O WELB
BRUCE R BAXTER · JOHN W BROOK
DENNIS E HILL · ROBERT L DEVOE ·
ROBERT C L FERGUSSON · CLINTON
AUGHN M HINES · HENRY R HOO
HN M KAPELUCK · DONALD M K
ROBERT MATTHEWS Jr · RICHARD A
RONALD P PRINCE · DOUGLAS E SC
GARY W SCHMITT · THOMAS L SCO
KENNETH W TINGLE · WILLIAM A W
LARRY J BAKER · STEPHEN D BARTEL
STEPHEN H BYLER · TERRY LEE CLAR
ROBERT R GONNEVILLE · EDWIN M
RICHARD M HOOTS · JAMES R HOV
ROBERT L JOHNSON Jr · ROBERT L H
ROBERT F NITZ · DENNIS R PODGO
PETER A SCHRADER · GARY LEE REH
BILLY TEMPLETON · FREDDIE LEE TH
CHARLES E WEAVER · JAMES C WHI
MICHAEL A HOGLUND · WILLIAM H
JAMES A CREW · CHARLES W CRIZZ
LUIS BARRETO Jr · CHARLES J HUNE
NORMAN J LIVINGSTON · CLIFFOR
WILLIAM T BROCK · ALFRED TIMMS
FRANCIS D BATTISTA · JAMES L BEYE
JAMES A COLLIER · JOHN J COLLINS
JOHN P FALCONE Jr · ROBERT R GRC
JOHN W HILL III · GREGORY J DELLA
GLENN D KERNS · LARRY MARTIN ·
JAMES H McCRAE · CARL J McHANE
JIMMIE DALE ROGERS · CHARLES D
GEORGE E STIVERS · JOHN S STUCK

Lin resisted. She said The Wall would tell the story of each battle in the war if the names were listed by years. Soldiers who fought and died together would be together in the listings. This would make the Memorial more personal, she said.

More importantly, Lin didn't want the Memorial to look like a stone telephone book. More than 600 men named Smith died in the war. Many soldiers had the same first and last names. Listing by years would help identify these people as individuals.

Arguments about the design continued. Some organizers were afraid that if no one could agree, the Memorial itself would be put off—maybe for years. They had to find a way to agree.

A military official finally suggested placing a statue nearby as a more traditional element to the Memorial. At last, everyone agreed—except Maya Lin. This was her design, she protested. She didn't want a statue added to it.

A Compromise

Although the names of veterans are listed on the wall according to the year they died, there is a directory of names to assist visitors to The Wall. This directory contains a list of the names in alphabetical order. With each name is the number of the panel and line on The Wall where the soldier's name can be found.

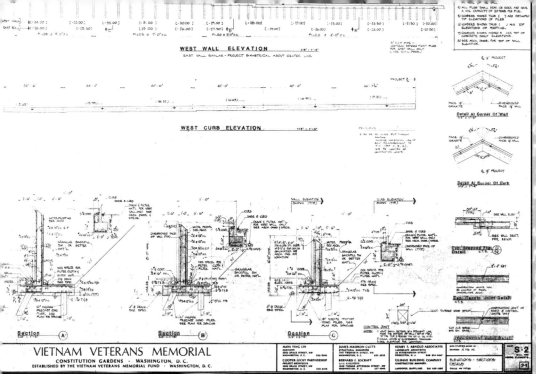

Architectural plans for the Memorial

But building soon began on The Wall *and* the statue. And the Memorial opened on Veterans Day in 1982, just the way Jan Scruggs had hoped. And, despite everyone's worries, The Wall affected Americans the way he'd hoped it would.

Words About The Wall

Lin made rare comments about her work on November 11, 1992. She attended the tenth anniversary ceremony for The Wall on that Veterans Day.

"Oftentimes, I just let the work speak for itself, but I really wanted to come back here for the 10th Anniversary," she said. "It has meant a lot for me to have done something that can help so many. I feel I might be the author, but I would like to remain fairly silent. The Wall is designed for you, for everyone to come and bring their thoughts, their emotions to The Wall. You make it come alive. And I want to thank all of you for your service to this country. Thank you very much."

Chapter Six

A Day at the Wall

More than four million people visit the Vietnam Veterans Memorial each year. Many visitors leave something behind.

People leave letters to individual names on The Wall. The letters often express appreciation for the veterans and tell what has happened since they died.

Sometimes, friends and family members leave something special from a serviceperson's past. It might be an item from that person's tour of duty in Vietnam. It might be a memento from the soldier's childhood or life before the war.

In the summer of 1982, a U.S. Navy officer walked up to the **trench** where the concrete foundation of The Wall was being poured. He stood over the trench for a moment and then tossed something in and saluted. A workman asked the man what he was doing. The officer said he was giving his dead brother's Purple Heart to The Wall.

Purple Heart

The Purple Heart is a medal awarded to any soldier who has been killed or injured in an armed conflict.

Since then, the National Park Service (NPS) has saved more than 64,000 **artifacts** left at The Wall. More than 1,500 new items are left at The Wall each month. Each day, all offerings are gathered and saved by NPS workers or volunteers. They note by which of the 70 panels the item was left because many items are left for a specific name.

Name Rubbings

While many come to leave gifts, they often take something away too. Volunteers are always at The Wall with paper, ready to help people make rubbings of a cherished name. By placing a sheet of paper over a name and rubbing a crayon across the paper, a soldier's name can be taken home.

Names on The Wall

The names on The Wall move in a cycle. They begin in the middle of the V shape with deaths that occurred in 1959. The names move to the right until that part of The Wall (the east panel) ends. Then the names continue on The Wall's left (or west) panel. The names on the west panel begin on the outside panel and move right until they reach the middle. Here, the final deaths from 1975 connect to the first in 1959. Through 16 years and thousands of deaths, the lives become united.

If records show that a Vietnam death was overlooked, that person's name will be engraved on The Wall. Names are added in May before Memorial Day. Extra space near the edges of each panel allows new names to continue being listed by the dates of their deaths. In 2002, three more names were added. The total listed on The Wall grew to 58,229 names.

Mementos left at The Wall

The Gift of Healing

Visitors to The Wall are united too with memories of people they loved. Standing together at the Memorial, they can share their joyful memories and their sad losses. Often it helps friends and families to know that they are not alone.

Although many visitors to The Wall leave gifts behind, they often receive a gift in return. It is the gift of healing.

Special Days at The Wall

Other special events take place at The Wall throughout the year. Ceremonies are held on Veterans Day, Mother's Day, and Father's Day. Visitors gather to watch the flying of the flag, enjoy patriotic music, and listen to speakers.

President Ronald Reagan and First Lady Nancy Reagan visit The Wall in 1984.

Chapter Seven

The Wall ❧ Reaches Out

People who can't go to Washington, D.C., can still experience The Wall thanks to several traveling **replicas**. Although they are much smaller than the original Wall, these replicas still contain all the names of the deceased soldiers.

The Man Behind the Traveling Wall

John Devitt was the first to dream of putting The Wall on tour.

After Devitt graduated from high school, he thought about attending college, but he enlisted in the army instead. Devitt worked as a helicopter gunner in Vietnam. He was shot down by enemy gunfire three times. Engine failure crashed his helicopter a fourth time.

When he returned home to California in 1969, Devitt wanted to forget the things he had seen during the war. But his friends wanted him to see the unveiling of The Wall in 1982. They treated him to a plane ticket to Washington, D.C.

Like many veterans, Devitt was unsure about going to a place that would bring back painful memories. But after seeing The Wall, Devitt no longer felt alone with his memories. He once again felt proud for having served his country. He wanted other veterans to feel that way too.

ALPH L AVERY · ROBERT J BICKEL · CHARLES G BOWERSMITH · PAUL F BRO
OAQUIN PALACIOS CABRERA · ROBERT I CARTER · JAMES L JENKINS · ROBE
JIMMY E FLOREN · AF
· THOMAS G HAWK
AN L JONES · EMORY
G · WALTER W LEWV
LER Jr · JOHN R NO
LD F SANSONE · JO

Devitt thought that facing the past might be easier for a veteran if he could be in a familiar place with familiar people. What if The Wall could travel to veterans' communities?

Building the Moving Wall

Devitt decided to rebuild The Wall in a smaller size and take it to the people. He and his friends combined their savings. They had only $2,500. They thought they'd need at least $40,000. Then companies started helping. Soon, Devitt's group was able to create its moving wall.

The first movable wall was made of lightweight **Plexiglas** panels. Later, the panels were aluminum. Names were **silk-screened** on the panels. The Vietnam Veterans Memorial Fund provided **negative** copies of each name from the actual Wall, assuring that the exhibit would look like the real thing.

Just like in Washington, D.C., many visitors to The Moving Wall exhibit leave notes and other mementos to honor those who served.

The first Moving Wall exhibit appeared in 1984. A second identical exhibit is now available, helping to reach more people in more places. Countries as far away as Ireland and Guam have hosted Devitt's dream.

Volunteers finish the lighting setup for The Moving Wall exhibit.

JNTER · MAX RIDO
LARRY W MAYSEY · R
GWICK · TOMAS GA
ELL · LARRY D SHARP
TICHENOR · PHILIP F
NTERS · TYRONE W
AYMOND H CHASE · I
DING · ARTHUR L H

The Wall That Heals

The Vietnam Veterans Fund unveiled another replica wall on Veterans Day, 1996. The Wall That Heals traveling exhibit includes a replica of The Wall and a museum with eight display cases of war artifacts and mementos left as tributes at the Washington, D.C., Memorial. It also has an Information Center where visitors can look up names of people on The Wall.

The Virtual Wall

As The Moving Wall and The Wall That Heals travel America, another Wall is traveling in cyberspace. The Vietnam Veterans Memorial Fund uses the Internet to tell the story of the war and the Memorial. The Virtual Wall Web site (www.thevirtualwall.org) has more than one million viewers per month.

Internet visitors can print an electronic name rubbing from a name found on The Wall. They can also leave written messages, photos, or even audio memories for anyone listed on the Memorial. With the aid of the Web site, the Vietnam Veterans Memorial Fund has begun a program called "Put a Face with a Name." The Memorial Fund is trying to collect a photo for every name listed on The Wall.

Traveling exhibits bring The Wall to cities around the world. The Internet provides instant access to the Memorial from people's homes. In Washington, D.C., and across the country, the stories of the men and women who served in Vietnam live on.

Visitors at The Moving Wall exhibit

Names with Faces

The Vietnam Veterans Memorial is more than The Wall. Two statues honor those who served and give faces to the names of those who died.

Three Servicemen

Three Servicemen is a bronze sculpture by Frederick E. Hart. The statue was added to the Memorial on Veterans Day, 1984. The sculpture shows three soldiers standing together. One man is Caucasian. One is Hispanic. One is African American.

The artist wanted the statues to relate to The Wall. "I see The Wall as a kind of ocean, a sea of sacrifice that is overwhelming and nearly **incomprehensible** in its sweep of names," Hart said. "I place these figures upon the shore of that sea, gazing upon it, standing **vigil** before it, reflecting the human face of it, the human heart."

Hart's involvement with the Vietnam Veterans Memorial started early.

"In 1979, I read a letter to the editor by a Vietnam veteran who was proposing a memorial to the Vietnam War," Hart said. "I was immediately intrigued and electrified by the idea, so I got in touch with him. From the very beginning I was involved in the project."

When the idea of a national contest was finally chosen, Hart was disappointed. He felt that such a huge contest was "so much like a lottery."

But Hart "felt so strongly and passionately about the subject" that he entered anyway. He won third place and $5,000 for his design, but not the chance to build his dream.

At least, not at first.

"When they chose the design for The Wall, I thought the whole thing was over," Hart said. "There were a number of vets, however, who wanted something more." That something more was a statue and a flag. Soon, Hart was asked to create his statue.

His idea for the work flowed out "in the course of three hours . . . almost exactly as you see it here now," he said. "I think it's just one of those things that happens after three or four years of being intensely dedicated to a subject."

Flying the Flag

In addition to Hart's *Three Servicemen* statue, an American flag was added to the Memorial site.

The Vietnam Women's Memorial

Approximately 265,000 women were enlisted in the armed forces during the time of the Vietnam War. About 11,000 of these women served time in Vietnam. Most of the women were nurses, but others were doctors, physical therapists, air traffic controllers, and other military workers.

The Vietnam Women's Memorial Project was formed to honor and support the women who served in Vietnam. It encourages the healing of both the women and their families and continues to identify the names of women who served. Currently, the names of eight women who died in Vietnam are recognized on The Wall.

Glenna Goodacre sculpted the Vietnam Women's Memorial. The statue was dedicated on Veterans Day, 1993.

The Women's Memorial shows one nurse holding a wounded soldier in her arms. Another nurse is scanning the sky as if looking for a helicopter, the flying ambulance of the war. "Or, perhaps," said Goodacre, "she's in search of help from God." A third nurse is kneeling behind the others holding an empty helmet in her hands. All three women were designed to reflect the emotional effects of the war.

The nurses are centered around a pile of sandbags. Goodacre said that she saw a lot of pictures from the war that contained sandbags. She built her memorial around the idea that the sandbags were supporting the women who had supported the soldiers in the war.

In Honor of Women

Glenna Goodacre is known for her works honoring women. In addition to the Vietnam Women's Memorial, she also created the design for the one-dollar gold coin of Sacagawea.

This replica of the Women's Memorial is located in the Pentagon in Washington, D.C.

The Future of the Memorial

The idea behind a memorial is to keep memories alive. Memorials help unite the past, present, and future. For although memorials honor the dead, they are made for the living. And life is always changing. That's why the Vietnam Veterans Memorial keeps changing too.

Plans for the Future

The Memorial Fund hopes to build an underground visitor education center near The Wall. The center would tell the story of how The Wall was built and how it has affected veterans and others who have visited it.

Internet Connections to the Vietnam Veterans Memorial

http://www.vvmf.org
This is the site of the organization that led the fund-raising for The Wall. Check here for news about The Wall That Heals, the traveling Wall replica that might someday visit a town near you.

http://www.thevirtualwall.org
This site is the next best thing to being at the Memorial in Washington, D.C. You can look up the name of someone from your hometown. You can see a virtual name rubbing and remembrances that have been left at The Wall. Soldiers, friends, and family have posted photos, stories, and recordings about veterans.

http://www.vietnamwomensmemorial.org
Learn about the role that women played in the Vietnam War, and experience the memorial that honors them.

http://www.sdit.org
This is the Web site for Sons and Daughters In Touch (SDIT). This group was formed to lend support to all those whose fathers died while serving in Vietnam. SDIT estimates that 20,000 American children became fatherless because of Vietnam deaths.

http://vets.appliedphysics.swri.edu/interviews/index.htm
Vietnam veterans have volunteered to answer questions from students online. Questions and answers are posted on this Web site so that everyone may share and learn.

ambush	surprise attack
artifact	something created by humans for a specific purpose
combat	active fighting in a war
communism	system where the government owns all businesses and industries
Communist	relating to communism (see separate entry for *communism*); person who believes in communism
comrade	fellow soldier
contemplative	causing people to think of, pray for, or honor
corporal	person in the military who ranks below a sergeant
deferment	official postponement, or delay, in military service
democracy	system where government officials are elected by the people and private ownership of businesses and industries exists
draft	process of requiring citizens to serve in the military

drafted	required to serve in the military
enlist	to sign up for military service
exempt	freed or released from a requirement
foreign	relating to a country other than one's own
granite	very hard rock with visible crystals
harmonious	blending or fitting in with
incomprehensible	not understandable
infantryman	soldier trained, armed, and equipped to fight on foot
majesty	greatness; magnificence
national	relating to the whole country
negative	photographic image used for printing pictures
neutral	not taking sides in a war
pacifist	person who is opposed to violence and war
patriotism	love for and devotion to one's country
Plexiglas	sheets of plastic

political	relating to the way the government runs a country
replica	exact copy
rifleman	soldier armed with a rifle
shrapnel	metal projectile that explodes in flight; pieces of such a projectile
silk-screened	to put color on a material
trench	long cut in the ground
truce	temporary or permanent stop in fighting
unit	group of soldiers
veteran	person who was a member of the military
vigil	watch